PCPC Daily Prayer Guide, No. 17, © 2020 Park Cities Presbyterian Church.
All rights reserved

Unless otherwise indicated, Scripture quotations are from *ESV© Bible (The Holy Bible, English Standard Version©)*, Copyright 2001 by Crossway Bibles, a publishing ministry of Good News Publishers. Used by permission. All rights reserved.

Park Cities Presbyterian Church
4124 Oak Lawn Avenue, Dallas, Texas 75219
pcpc.org | 214-224-2500

PARK CITIES PRESBYTERIAN CHURCH
DAILY PRAYER GUIDE

ADVENT & CHRISTMAS 2020

And the Word became flesh and dwelt among us, and we have seen his glory, glory as of the only Son from the Father, full of grace and truth.

JOHN 1:14

TABLE OF CONTENTS

INTRODUCTION.................................. 7-9

PRAYER GUIDE.................................. 10-85

APPENDIX... 86-87

    APOSTLES' CREED......................... 86

    LORD'S PRAYER............................. 87

    A WAY OF PERSONAL EXAMINATION.... 87

NOTES... 88-89

PCPC PRAYER GUIDE INTRODUCTION

This guide has a simple aim: to help us grow in our love for God through time in His Word and prayer. The Bible teaches that in order to love God, we need a relationship with Him. Though we had caused alienation from God by our sin, God Himself has nevertheless provided for that relationship in His overcoming the alienation through the life, death, and resurrection of Jesus Christ, who is God the Son. In union with Christ, we now have intimate access to God as our heavenly Father. Scripture and prayer are the means through which we experience, apply, and enjoy that relationship. As we learn to pray, and as we learn to listen and obey the gracious overtures of God's Word, we learn to live as God's children, loving and trusting Him more fully.

WHY DAILY PRAYER?

Why set aside fixed times every day for prayer? Why not simply pray unprompted, when the stirring comes? Practically speaking, we are creatures attuned to rhythms. We order our lives by sunrises and sunsets, by hours, weeks, seasons, and years. Daily prayer is a way of consecrating our ordinary rhythms to God, ensuring that all of life is offered to Him. C. S. Lewis once wrote, "Relying on God has to begin all over again every day as if nothing had yet been done." And so it must. Our relationship with God should take hold of our schedules, as well as our hearts.

WHY A PRAYER GUIDE?

Here are a few compelling reasons to use a prayer guide:

1. It helps us to pray regularly.

Sometimes we may not pray regularly because we may not know where to begin. A prayer guide takes the pressure off needing to make that decision anew every day. It repeatedly says, "Start here" and let God's Word lead you into prayer.

2. It helps us to pray biblically.

The majority of the reading is from Scripture. We will read through the Psalms, a book of the Bible meant especially for prayer and worship. One of the encouraging messages reiterated in the Psalms is that you do not have to put on a happy face to live the Christian life. Praying biblically allows us to pray the truth of who we are while growing in the hope of who we might yet become.

3. It helps us to pray communally.

Though we are praying individually, we are doing so together, specifically as a church body. This book is meant for this flock, in this time and place. To know that others with whom God has joined us are reading and praying the same words encourages us in our common journey. Prayer is a communal activity as much as an individual one.

HOW TO USE THIS GUIDE

Use this guide however may be helpful to you. For many, that means using it just as it is. For those who are in the habit of family worship, you can adapt the guide to read and pray together as a family.

Here are suggestions for each of the elements:

The Call to Worship

The Call to Worship is God's initiating with you through His Word. Read the call, perhaps out loud. Receive God's invitation to worship Him as spoken to you in that moment.

The Prayers of Praise and Thanksgiving

Praise God for who He is as He has shown in His Word and in your life. Thank Him for His presence and gifts in your life.

The Readings

Our Advent & Christmas Daily Prayer Guide theme is "The Word Became Flesh." Join us wherever you find yourself over Advent and Christmas as we read and pray together through the Psalms. Get to know the words here, and you will better know Jesus Himself. The other Scripture Readings for this season are drawn from various passages in the Old and New Testaments that outline the unfolding work of God's grace in redeeming a people for Himself. These passages establish our need for a Messiah and celebrate Jesus Christ as our Redeemer and King. May the story of God's Word fill us with a vibrant hope in Jesus Christ this Advent & Christmas season.

Questions for Meditation

We have given three questions to help create space and encouragement to listen and obey the Word of God. Use these questions to guide you as you go back to circle, highlight, or write notes in the margins.

Prayer of Confession

This is an opportunity to repent for the ways we have missed the mark and to receive the grace we need for renewal and change. Ask God for mercy. Ask Him to help you become more like Christ.

Prayer of Supplication

We will give a new opportunity each day for you to lift up people and ministries in our community and around the world. You may also layout before God whatever burdens you carry as well as those others carry.

Weekly Collect

The Weekly Collect is a way to conclude. All of the closing prayers draw from The Book of Common Prayer. They are called "collects" because they gather our prayers together and present them before God collectively as we go about our scattered lives. Pray this prayer as your own in the confidence that others are praying with you.

Sundays

Sundays are unique as our time to gather and worship as a church family, to celebrate once again the victory of Christ over sin and death. There are only Psalm readings on Sunday because the liturgy of corporate worship is our primary focus. We have added a page for sermon notes.

A Note for Families

This prayer guide can be a great tool for times of family worship. We suggest letting any of those who are able take turns reading each element. This ensures that everyone is involved in both hearing and speaking the Word of God with one another. During the Prayers of Praise and Thanksgiving, you may each say something aloud, no matter how short or clumsy (we are all learners!). During the Prayer of Confession, take a minute to pray to God personally in the quiet of your own thoughts. This is just one way to use the guide as a family. We encourage you to explore how it might best help your own worship and devotion in your life together.

As a final word, there are many great reading plans, devotionals, and exercises to encourage in us a life of prayer. This is a way to pray, only one among many that has grown up in the history of God's people. Most important is not the method, but the reality of loving and trusting God. May your relationship with Him grow.

SUNDAY, NOVEMBER 29

Psalm 92

> A Psalm. A Song for the Sabbath.
> 1 It is good to give thanks to the LORD,
>   to sing praises to your name, O Most High;
> 2 to declare your steadfast love in the morning,
>   and your faithfulness by night,
> 3 to the music of the lute and the harp,
>   to the melody of the lyre.
> 4 For you, O LORD, have made me glad by your work;
>   at the works of your hands I sing for joy.
> 5 How great are your works, O LORD!
>   Your thoughts are very deep!
> 6 The stupid man cannot know;
>   the fool cannot understand this:
> 7 that though the wicked sprout like grass
>   and all evildoers flourish,
> they are doomed to destruction forever;
> 8   but you, O LORD, are on high forever.
> 9 For behold, your enemies, O LORD,
>   for behold, your enemies shall perish;
>   all evildoers shall be scattered.
> 10 But you have exalted my horn like that of the wild ox;
>   you have poured over me fresh oil.
> 11 My eyes have seen the downfall of my enemies;
>   my ears have heard the doom of my evil assailants.
> 12 The righteous flourish like the palm tree
>   and grow like a cedar in Lebanon.
> 13 They are planted in the house of the LORD;
>   they flourish in the courts of our God.
> 14 They still bear fruit in old age;
>   they are ever full of sap and green,
> 15 to declare that the LORD is upright;
>   he is my rock, and there is no unrighteousness in him.

Sermon Notes

MONDAY, NOVEMBER 30

Call to Worship

17 The LORD is righteous in all his ways and kind in all his works.
18 The LORD is near to all who call on him, to all who call on him in truth.
(Psalm 145:17-18)

Prayers of Adoration and Thanksgiving

Psalm 1:1-2

1 Blessed is the man
   who walks not in the counsel of the wicked,
nor stands in the way of sinners,
   nor sits in the seat of scoffers;
2 but his delight is in the law of the LORD,
   and on his law he meditates day and night.

Scripture Reading: Genesis 3:1-15

1 Now the serpent was more crafty than any other beast of the field that the LORD God had made.

He said to the woman, "Did God actually say, 'You shall not eat of any tree in the garden'?" 2 And the woman said to the serpent, "We may eat of the fruit of the trees in the garden, 3 but God said, 'You shall not eat of the fruit of the tree that is in the midst of the garden, neither shall you touch it, lest you die.'" 4 But the serpent said to the woman, "You will not surely die. 5 For God knows that when you eat of it your eyes will be opened, and you will be like God, knowing good and evil." 6 So when the woman saw that the tree was good for food, and that it was a delight to the eyes, and that the tree was to be desired to make one wise, she took of its fruit and ate, and she also gave some to her husband who was with her, and he ate. 7 Then the eyes of both were opened, and they knew that they were naked. And they sewed fig leaves together and made themselves loincloths.

8 And they heard the sound of the LORD God walking in the garden in the cool of the day, and the man and his wife hid themselves from the presence of the LORD God among the trees of the garden. 9 But the LORD God called to the man and said to him, "Where are you?" 10 And he said, "I heard the sound of you in the garden, and I was afraid, because I was naked, and I hid myself." 11 He said, "Who told you that you were naked? Have you eaten of the tree of which I commanded you not to eat?" 12 The man said, "The woman whom you gave to be with me, she gave me fruit of the tree, and I ate." 13 Then the LORD God said to the woman, "What is this that you have done?" The woman said, "The serpent deceived me, and I ate."

14 The LORD God said to the serpent,

"Because you have done this, cursed are you above all livestock and above all beasts of the field; on your belly you shall go, and dust you shall eat all the days of your life.

15 I will put enmity between you and the woman, and between your offspring and her offspring; he shall bruise your head, and you shall bruise his heel."

Time of Reflection

What does God say in this passage that stands out to you?

What does it teach you about God and yourself?

How will you respond in faith and obedience today?

Prayer of Confession

Prayer of Supplication

Widows, elderly, and homebound in our church family

Weekly Collect

Almighty God, give us grace to cast away the works of darkness, and put on the armor of light, now in the time of this mortal life in which Your Son Jesus Christ came to visit us in great humility; that in the last day, when He shall come again in His glorious majesty to judge both the living and the dead, we may rise to the life immortal; through Him who lives and reigns with You and the Holy Spirit, one God, now and forever. *Amen.*

TUESDAY, DECEMBER 1

Call to Worship

> 5 Great is our Lord, and abundant in power; his understanding is beyond measure. (Psalm 147:5)

Prayers of Adoration and Thanksgiving

Psalm 1:3-6

> 3 He is like a tree
>   planted by streams of water
> that yields its fruit in its season,
>   and its leaf does not wither.
> In all that he does, he prospers.
> 4 The wicked are not so,
>   but are like chaff that the wind drives away.
> 5 Therefore the wicked will not stand in the judgment,
>   nor sinners in the congregation of the righteous;
> 6 for the LORD knows the way of the righteous,
>   but the way of the wicked will perish.

Scripture Reading: Isaiah 9:2-17

> 2 The people who walked in darkness have seen a great light; those who dwelt in a land of deep darkness, on them has light shone.
> 3 You have multiplied the nation; you have increased its joy; they rejoice before you as with joy at the harvest, as they are glad when they divide the spoil.
> 4 For the yoke of his burden, and the staff for his shoulder, the rod of his oppressor, you have broken as on the day of Midian.
> 5 For every boot of the tramping warrior in battle tumult and every garment rolled in blood will be burned as fuel for the fire.
> 6 For to us a child is born, to us a son is given; and the government shall be upon his shoulder, and his name shall be called Wonderful Counselor, Mighty God, Everlasting Father, Prince of Peace.
> 7 Of the increase of his government and of peace there will be no end, on the throne of David and over his kingdom, to establish it and to uphold it with justice and with righteousness from this time forth and forevermore. The zeal of the LORD of hosts will do this. Judgment on Arrogance and Oppression
> 8 The LORD has sent a word against Jacob, and it will fall on Israel;
> 9 and all the people will know, Ephraim and the inhabitants of Samaria, who say in pride and in arrogance of heart:
> 10 "The bricks have fallen, but we will build with dressed stones; the sycamores have been cut down, but we will put cedars in their place."
> 11 But the LORD raises the adversaries of Rezin against him, and stirs up his enemies.

12 The Syrians on the east and the Philistines on the west devour Israel with open mouth. For all this his anger has not turned away, and his hand is stretched out still.
13 The people did not turn to him who struck them, nor inquire of the LORD of hosts.
14 So the LORD cut off from Israel head and tail, palm branch and reed in one day—
15 the elder and honored man is the head, and the prophet who teaches lies is the tail;
16 for those who guide this people have been leading them astray, and those who are guided by them are swallowed up.
17 Therefore the LORD does not rejoice over their young men, and has no compassion on their fatherless and widows; for everyone is godless and an evildoer, and every mouth speaks folly. For all this his anger has not turned away, and his hand is stretched out still.

Time of Reflection

What does God say in this passage that stands out to you?

What does it teach you about God and yourself?

How will you respond in faith and obedience today?

Prayer of Confession

Prayer of Supplication

Healing and reconciliation in broken relationships

Weekly Collect

Almighty God, give us grace to cast away the works of darkness, and put on the armor of light, now in the time of this mortal life in which Your Son Jesus Christ came to visit us in great humility; that in the last day, when He shall come again in His glorious majesty to judge both the living and the dead, we may rise to the life immortal; through Him who lives and reigns with You and the Holy Spirit, one God, now and forever. *Amen.*

WEDNESDAY, DECEMBER 2

Call to Worship

> 4 For the LORD takes pleasure in his people; he adorns the humble with salvation. 5 Let the godly exult in glory; let them sing for joy on their beds. (Psalm 149:4-5)

Prayers of Adoration and Thanksgiving

Psalm 2:1-6

> 1 Why do the nations rage
>   and the peoples plot in vain?
> 2 The kings of the earth set themselves,
>   and the rulers take counsel together,
>   against the LORD and against his Anointed, saying,
> 3 "Let us burst their bonds apart
>   and cast away their cords from us."
> 4 He who sits in the heavens laughs;
>   the LORD holds them in derision.
> 5 Then he will speak to them in his wrath,
>   and terrify them in his fury, saying,
> 6 "As for me, I have set my King
>   on Zion, my holy hill."

Scripture Reading: Isaiah 11:1-9

> 1 There shall come forth a shoot from the stump of Jesse,
>   and a branch from his roots shall bear fruit.
> 2 And the Spirit of the LORD shall rest upon him,
>   the Spirit of wisdom and understanding,
>   the Spirit of counsel and might,
>   the Spirit of knowledge and the fear of the LORD.
> 3 And his delight shall be in the fear of the LORD.
> He shall not judge by what his eyes see,
>   or decide disputes by what his ears hear,
> 4 but with righteousness he shall judge the poor,
>   and decide with equity for the meek of the earth;
> and he shall strike the earth with the rod of his mouth,
>   and with the breath of his lips he shall kill the wicked.
> 5 Righteousness shall be the belt of his waist,
>   and faithfulness the belt of his loins.
> 6 The wolf shall dwell with the lamb,
>   and the leopard shall lie down with the young goat,
> and the calf and the lion and the fattened calf together;
>   and a little child shall lead them.
> 7 The cow and the bear shall graze;
>   their young shall lie down together;
>   and the lion shall eat straw like the ox.

8 The nursing child shall play over the hole of the cobra,
   and the weaned child shall put his hand on the adder's den.
9 They shall not hurt or destroy
   in all my holy mountain;
for the earth shall be full of the knowledge of the LORD
   as the waters cover the sea.

Time of Reflection

What does God say in this passage that stands out to you?

What does it teach you about God and yourself?

How will you respond in faith and obedience today?

Prayer of Confession

Prayer of Supplication

Families who have lost loved ones this year

Weekly Collect

Almighty God, give us grace to cast away the works of darkness, and put on the armor of light, now in the time of this mortal life in which Your Son Jesus Christ came to visit us in great humility; that in the last day, when He shall come again in His glorious majesty to judge both the living and the dead, we may rise to the life immortal; through Him who lives and reigns with You and the Holy Spirit, one God, now and forever. *Amen.*

THURSDAY, DECEMBER 3

Call to Worship

4 Behold, God is my helper; the LORD is the upholder of my life. (Psalm 54:4)

Prayers of Adoration and Thanksgiving

Psalm 2:7-12

7 I will tell of the decree:
The LORD said to me, "You are my Son;
   today I have begotten you.
8 Ask of me, and I will make the nations your heritage,
   and the ends of the earth your possession.
9 You shall break them with a rod of iron
   and dash them in pieces like a potter's vessel."
10 Now therefore, O kings, be wise;
   be warned, O rulers of the earth.
11 Serve the LORD with fear,
   and rejoice with trembling.
12 Kiss the Son,
   lest he be angry, and you perish in the way,
   for his wrath is quickly kindled.
Blessed are all who take refuge in him.

Scripture Reading: Micah 5:2-4

2 But you, O Bethlehem Ephrathah,
who are too little to be among the clans of Judah,
from you shall come forth for me
one who is to be ruler in Israel,
whose coming forth is from of old,
from ancient days.
3 Therefore he shall give them up until the time
when she who is in labor has given birth;
then the rest of his brothers shall return
to the people of Israel.
4 And he shall stand and shepherd his flock in the strength of the LORD,
in the majesty of the name of the LORD his God.
And they shall dwell secure, for now he shall be great
to the ends of the earth.

Time of Reflection

    What does God say in this passage that stands out to you?

    What does it teach you about God and yourself?

    How will you respond in faith and obedience today?

Prayer of Confession

Prayer of Supplication

    Homeless in our city

Weekly Collect

    Almighty God, give us grace to cast away the works of darkness, and put on the armor of light, now in the time of this mortal life in which Your Son Jesus Christ came to visit us in great humility; that in the last day, when He shall come again in His glorious majesty to judge both the living and the dead, we may rise to the life immortal; through Him who lives and reigns with You and the Holy Spirit, one God, now and forever. *Amen.*

FRIDAY, DECEMBER 4

Call to Worship

8 Let all the earth fear the LORD; let all the inhabitants of the world stand in awe of him! (Psalm 33:8)

Prayers of Adoration and Thanksgiving

Psalm 103:1-5

1 Bless the LORD, O my soul,
  and all that is within me,
  bless his holy name!
2 Bless the LORD, O my soul,
  and forget not all his benefits,
3 who forgives all your iniquity,
  who heals all your diseases,
4 who redeems your life from the pit,
  who crowns you with steadfast love and mercy,
5 who satisfies you with good
  so that your youth is renewed like the eagle's.

Scripture Reading: Isaiah 53

1 Who has believed what he has heard from us?
And to whom has the arm of the LORD been revealed?
2 For he grew up before him like a young plant, and like a root out of dry ground;
he had no form or majesty that we should look at him, and no beauty that we should desire him.
3 He was despised and rejected by men, a man of sorrows and acquainted with grief;
and as one from whom men hide their faces he was despised, and we esteemed him not.
4 Surely he has borne our griefs and carried our sorrows;
yet we esteemed him stricken, smitten by God, and afflicted.
5 But he was pierced for our transgressions;
he was crushed for our iniquities;
upon him was the chastisement that brought us peace,
and with his wounds we are healed.
6 All we like sheep have gone astray;
we have turned—every one—to his own way;
and the LORD has laid on him the iniquity of us all.
7 He was oppressed, and he was afflicted, yet he opened not his mouth;
like a lamb that is led to the slaughter,
and like a sheep that before its shearers is silent,
so he opened not his mouth.
8 By oppression and judgment he was taken away;
and as for his generation, who considered

that he was cut off out of the land of the living,
stricken for the transgression of my people?
9 And they made his grave with the wicked and with a rich man in his death,
although he had done no violence, and there was no deceit in his mouth.
10 Yet it was the will of the LORD to crush him; he has put him to grief;
when his soul makes an offering for guilt,
he shall see his offspring; he shall prolong his days;
the will of the LORD shall prosper in his hand.
11 Out of the anguish of his soul he shall see and be satisfied;
by his knowledge shall the righteous one, my servant,
make many to be accounted righteous, and he shall bear their iniquities.
12 Therefore I will divide him a portion with the many,
and he shall divide the spoil with the strong,
because he poured out his soul to death and was numbered with the transgressors;
yet he bore the sin of many, and makes intercession for the transgressors.

Time of Reflection

What does God say in this passage that stands out to you?

What does it teach you about God and yourself?

How will you respond in faith and obedience today?

Prayer of Confession

Prayer of Supplication

Sick and suffering in our city

Weekly Collect

Almighty God, give us grace to cast away the works of darkness, and put on the armor of light, now in the time of this mortal life in which Your Son Jesus Christ came to visit us in great humility; that in the last day, when He shall come again in His glorious majesty to judge both the living and the dead, we may rise to the life immortal; through Him who lives and reigns with You and the Holy Spirit, one God, now and forever. *Amen.*

SATURDAY, DECEMBER 5

Call to Worship

5 For God alone, O my soul, wait in silence, for my hope is from him. (Psalm 62:5)

Prayers of Adoration and Thanksgiving

Psalm 103:6-10

6 The LORD works righteousness
   and justice for all who are oppressed.
7 He made known his ways to Moses,
   his acts to the people of Israel.
8 The LORD is merciful and gracious,
   slow to anger and abounding in steadfast love.
9 He will not always chide,
   nor will he keep his anger forever.
10 He does not deal with us according to our sins,
   nor repay us according to our iniquities.

Scripture Reading: Malachi 4

1 "For behold, the day is coming, burning like an oven, when all the arrogant and all evildoers will be stubble. The day that is coming shall set them ablaze, says the LORD of hosts, so that it will leave them neither root nor branch. 2 But for you who fear my name, the sun of righteousness shall rise with healing in its wings. You shall go out leaping like calves from the stall. 3 And you shall tread down the wicked, for they will be ashes under the soles of your feet, on the day when I act, says the LORD of hosts.

4 "Remember the law of my servant Moses, the statutes and rules that I commanded him at Horeb for all Israel.

5 "Behold, I will send you Elijah the prophet before the great and awesome day of the LORD comes. 6 And he will turn the hearts of fathers to their children and the hearts of children to their fathers, lest I come and strike the land with a decree of utter destruction."

Time of Reflection

What does God say in this passage that stands out to you?

What does it teach you about God and yourself?

How will you respond in faith and obedience today?

Prayer of Confession

Prayer of Supplication
>Orphans in our city

Weekly Collect
>Almighty God, give us grace to cast away the works of darkness, and put on the armor of light, now in the time of this mortal life in which Your Son Jesus Christ came to visit us in great humility; that in the last day, when He shall come again in His glorious majesty to judge both the living and the dead, we may rise to the life immortal; through Him who lives and reigns with You and the Holy Spirit, one God, now and forever. *Amen.*

SUNDAY, DECEMBER 6

Psalm 92

    A Psalm. A Song for the Sabbath.
1 It is good to give thanks to the LORD,
    to sing praises to your name, O Most High;
2 to declare your steadfast love in the morning,
    and your faithfulness by night,
3 to the music of the lute and the harp,
    to the melody of the lyre.
4 For you, O LORD, have made me glad by your work;
    at the works of your hands I sing for joy.
5 How great are your works, O LORD!
    Your thoughts are very deep!
6 The stupid man cannot know;
    the fool cannot understand this:
7 that though the wicked sprout like grass
    and all evildoers flourish,
they are doomed to destruction forever;
8   but you, O LORD, are on high forever.
9 For behold, your enemies, O LORD,
    for behold, your enemies shall perish;
    all evildoers shall be scattered.
10 But you have exalted my horn like that of the wild ox;
    you have poured over me fresh oil.
11 My eyes have seen the downfall of my enemies;
    my ears have heard the doom of my evil assailants.
12 The righteous flourish like the palm tree
    and grow like a cedar in Lebanon.
13 They are planted in the house of the LORD;
    they flourish in the courts of our God.
14 They still bear fruit in old age;
    they are ever full of sap and green,
15 to declare that the LORD is upright;
    he is my rock, and there is no unrighteousness in him.

Sermon Notes

MONDAY, DECEMBER 7

Call to Worship

27 The LORD is God,
and he has made his light to shine upon us.
Bind the festal sacrifice with cords,
up to the horns of the altar!
(Psalm 118:27)

Prayers of Adoration and Thanksgiving

Psalm 103:11-19

11 For as high as the heavens are above the earth,
   so great is his steadfast love toward those who fear him;
12 as far as the east is from the west,
   so far does he remove our transgressions from us.
13 As a father shows compassion to his children,
   so the LORD shows compassion to those who fear him.
14 For he knows our frame;
   he remembers that we are dust.

15 As for man, his days are like grass;
   he flourishes like a flower of the field;
16 for the wind passes over it, and it is gone,
   and its place knows it no more.
17 But the steadfast love of the LORD is from everlasting to everlasting
on those who fear him,
   and his righteousness to children's children,
18 to those who keep his covenant
   and remember to do his commandments.
19 The LORD has established his throne in the heavens,
   and his kingdom rules over all.

Scripture Reading: Genesis 12:1-3, 7; Galatians 3:15-16

1 Now the LORD said to Abram, "Go from your country and your kindred and your father's house to the land that I will show you. 2 And I will make of you a great nation, and I will bless you and make your name great, so that you will be a blessing. 3 I will bless those who bless you, and him who dishonors you I will curse, and in you all the families of the earth shall be blessed."

7 Then the LORD appeared to Abram and said, "To your offspring I will give this land." So he built there an altar to the LORD, who had appeared to him.

Galatians 3:15-16

15 To give a human example, brothers: even with a man-made covenant, no one annuls it or adds to it once it has been ratified. 16 Now the promises were made to Abraham and to his offspring. It does not say, "And to offsprings," referring to many, but referring to one, "And to your offspring," who is Christ.

Time of Reflection

What does God say in this passage that stands out to you?

What does it teach you about God and yourself?

How will you respond in faith and obedience today?

Prayer of Confession

Prayer of Supplication

Your family

Weekly Collect

Merciful God, who sent Your messengers the prophets to preach repentance and prepare the way for our salvation: Give us grace to heed their warnings and forsake our sins, that we may greet with joy the coming of Jesus Christ our Redeemer; who lives and reigns with You and the Holy Spirit, one God, now and forever. *Amen.*

TUESDAY, DECEMBER 8

Call to Worship

> 5 I wait for the LORD, my soul waits, and in his word I hope…
> (Psalm 130:5)

Prayers of Adoration and Thanksgiving

Psalm 119:174-176

> 174 I long for your salvation, O LORD,
>   and your law is my delight.
> 175 Let my soul live and praise you,
>   and let your rules help me.
> 176 I have gone astray like a lost sheep; seek your servant,
>   for I do not forget your commandments.

Scripture Reading: Exodus 20:1-17

> 1 And God spoke all these words, saying,
> 2 "I am the LORD your God, who brought you out of the land of Egypt, out of the house of slavery.
> 3 "You shall have no other gods before me.
> 4 "You shall not make for yourself a carved image, or any likeness of anything that is in heaven above, or that is in the earth beneath, or that is in the water under the earth. 5 You shall not bow down to them or serve them, for I the LORD your God am a jealous God, visiting the iniquity of the fathers on the children to the third and the fourth generation of those who hate me, 6 but showing steadfast love to thousands of those who love me and keep my commandments.
> 7 "You shall not take the name of the LORD your God in vain, for the LORD will not hold him guiltless who takes his name in vain.
> 8 "Remember the Sabbath day, to keep it holy. 9 Six days you shall labor, and do all your work, 10 but the seventh day is a Sabbath to the LORD your God. On it you shall not do any work, you, or your son, or your daughter, your male servant, or your female servant, or your livestock, or the sojourner who is within your gates. 11 For in six days the LORD made heaven and earth, the sea, and all that is in them, and rested on the seventh day. Therefore the LORD blessed the Sabbath day and made it holy.
> 12 "Honor your father and your mother, that your days may be long in the land that the LORD your God is giving you.
> 13 "You shall not murder.
> 14 "You shall not commit adultery.
> 15 "You shall not steal.
> 16 "You shall not bear false witness against your neighbor.
> 17 "You shall not covet your neighbor's house; you shall not covet your neighbor's wife, or his male servant, or his female servant, or his ox, or his donkey, or anything that is your neighbor's."

Time of Reflection

    What does God say in this passage that stands out to you?

    What does it teach you about God and yourself?

    How will you respond in faith and obedience today?

Prayer of Confession

Prayer of Supplication

    Your neighbors

Weekly Collect

    Merciful God, who sent Your messengers the prophets to preach repentance and prepare the way for our salvation: Give us grace to heed their warnings and forsake our sins, that we may greet with joy the coming of Jesus Christ our Redeemer; who lives and reigns with You and the Holy Spirit, one God, now and forever. *Amen.*

WEDNESDAY, DECEMBER 9

Call to Worship

12 I give thanks to you, O LORD my God, with my whole heart, and I will glorify your name forever. (Psalm 86:12)

Prayers of Adoration and Thanksgiving

Psalm 23

1 The LORD is my shepherd; I shall not want.
2   He makes me lie down in green pastures.
He leads me beside still waters.
3   He restores my soul.
He leads me in paths of righteousness
    for his name's sake.
4 Even though I walk through the valley of the shadow of death,
    I will fear no evil,
for you are with me;
    your rod and your staff,
    they comfort me.
5 You prepare a table before me
    in the presence of my enemies;
you anoint my head with oil;
    my cup overflows.
6 Surely goodness and mercy shall follow me
    all the days of my life,
and I shall dwell in the house of the LORD
    forever.

Scripture Reading: Isaiah 40:1-11

1 Comfort, comfort my people, says your God.
2 Speak tenderly to Jerusalem,
and cry to her
that her warfare is ended,
that her iniquity is pardoned,
that she has received from the LORD's hand
double for all her sins.
3 A voice cries:
"In the wilderness prepare the way of the LORD;
make straight in the desert a highway for our God.
4 Every valley shall be lifted up,
and every mountain and hill be made low;
the uneven ground shall become level,
and the rough places a plain.
5 And the glory of the LORD shall be revealed,
and all flesh shall see it together,
for the mouth of the LORD has spoken."

6 A voice says, "Cry!"
And I said, "What shall I cry?"
All flesh is grass,
and all its beauty is like the flower of the field.
7 The grass withers, the flower fades
when the breath of the LORD blows on it;
surely the people are grass.
8 The grass withers, the flower fades,
but the word of our God will stand forever.
9 Go on up to a high mountain,
O Zion, herald of good news;
lift up your voice with strength,
O Jerusalem, herald of good news;
lift it up, fear not;
say to the cities of Judah,
"Behold your God!"
10 Behold, the LORD God comes with might,
and his arm rules for him;
behold, his reward is with him,
and his recompense before him.
11 He will tend his flock like a shepherd;
he will gather the lambs in his arms;
he will carry them in his bosom,
and gently lead those that are with young.

Time of Reflection

What does God say in this passage that stands out to you?

What does it teach you about God and yourself?

How will you respond in faith and obedience today?

Prayer of Confession

Prayer of Supplication

Your coworkers, classmates, and people you see every day

Weekly Collect

Merciful God, who sent Your messengers the prophets to preach repentance and prepare the way for our salvation: Give us grace to heed their warnings and forsake our sins, that we may greet with joy the coming of Jesus Christ our Redeemer; who lives and reigns with You and the Holy Spirit, one God, now and forever. *Amen.*

THURSDAY, DECEMBER 10

Call to Worship
> 10 All your works shall give thanks to you, O LORD,
> and all your saints shall bless you! (145:10)

Prayers of Adoration and Thanksgiving

Psalm 126
> 1 When the LORD restored the fortunes of Zion,
>   we were like those who dream.
> 2 Then our mouth was filled with laughter,
>   and our tongue with shouts of joy;
> then they said among the nations,
>   "The LORD has done great things for them."
> 3 The LORD has done great things for us;
>   we are glad.
> 4 Restore our fortunes, O LORD,
>   like streams in the Negeb!
> 5 Those who sow in tears
>   shall reap with shouts of joy!
> 6 He who goes out weeping,
>   bearing the seed for sowing,
> shall come home with shouts of joy,
>   bringing his sheaves with him.

Scripture Reading: Luke 1:5-25

5 In the days of Herod, king of Judea, there was a priest named Zechariah, of the division of Abijah. And he had a wife from the daughters of Aaron, and her name was Elizabeth. 6 And they were both righteous before God, walking blamelessly in all the commandments and statutes of the Lord. 7 But they had no child, because Elizabeth was barren, and both were advanced in years.

8 Now while he was serving as priest before God when his division was on duty, 9 according to the custom of the priesthood, he was chosen by lot to enter the temple of the Lord and burn incense. 10 And the whole multitude of the people were praying outside at the hour of incense. 11 And there appeared to him an angel of the Lord standing on the right side of the altar of incense. 12 And Zechariah was troubled when he saw him, and fear fell upon him. 13 But the angel said to him, "Do not be afraid, Zechariah, for your prayer has been heard, and your wife Elizabeth will bear you a son, and you shall call his name John. 14 And you will have joy and gladness, and many will rejoice at his birth, 15 for he will be great before the Lord. And he must not drink wine or strong drink, and he will be filled with the Holy Spirit, even from his mother's womb. 16 And

he will turn many of the children of Israel to the Lord their God, 17 and he will go before him in the spirit and power of Elijah, to turn the hearts of the fathers to the children, and the disobedient to the wisdom of the just, to make ready for the Lord a people prepared."

18 And Zechariah said to the angel, "How shall I know this? For I am an old man, and my wife is advanced in years." 19 And the angel answered him, "I am Gabriel. I stand in the presence of God, and I was sent to speak to you and to bring you this good news. 20 And behold, you will be silent and unable to speak until the day that these things take place, because you did not believe my words, which will be fulfilled in their time." 21 And the people were waiting for Zechariah, and they were wondering at his delay in the temple. 22 And when he came out, he was unable to speak to them, and they realized that he had seen a vision in the temple. And he kept making signs to them and remained mute. 23 And when his time of service was ended, he went to his home.

24 After these days his wife Elizabeth conceived, and for five months she kept herself hidden, saying, 25 "Thus the Lord has done for me in the days when he looked on me, to take away my reproach among people.".

Time of Reflection

What does God say in this passage that stands out to you?

What does it teach you about God and yourself?

How will you respond in faith and obedience today?

Prayer of Confession

Prayer of Supplication

Your community group

Weekly Collect

Merciful God, who sent Your messengers the prophets to preach repentance and prepare the way for our salvation: Give us grace to heed their warnings and forsake our sins, that we may greet with joy the coming of Jesus Christ our Redeemer; who lives and reigns with You and the Holy Spirit, one God, now and forever. *Amen.*

FRIDAY, DECEMBER 11

Call to Worship

13 Your kingdom is an everlasting kingdom, and your dominion endures throughout all generations. [The LORD is faithful in all his words and kind in all his works.] (Psalm 145:13)

Prayers of Adoration and Thanksgiving

Psalm 123

1 To you I lift up my eyes,
　O you who are enthroned in the heavens!
2 Behold, as the eyes of servants
　look to the hand of their master,
as the eyes of a maidservant
　to the hand of her mistress,
so our eyes look to the LORD our God,
　till he has mercy upon us.
3 Have mercy upon us, O LORD, have mercy upon us,
　for we have had more than enough of contempt.
4 Our soul has had more than enough
　of the scorn of those who are at ease,
　of the contempt of the proud.

Scripture Reading: Luke 1:26-45

26 In the sixth month the angel Gabriel was sent from God to a city of Galilee named Nazareth, 27 to a virgin betrothed to a man whose name was Joseph, of the house of David. And the virgin's name was Mary. 28 And he came to her and said, "Greetings, O favored one, the Lord is with you!" 29 But she was greatly troubled at the saying, and tried to discern what sort of greeting this might be. 30 And the angel said to her, "Do not be afraid, Mary, for you have found favor with God. 31 And behold, you will conceive in your womb and bear a son, and you shall call his name Jesus. 32 He will be great and will be called the Son of the Most High. And the Lord God will give to him the throne of his father David, 33 and he will reign over the house of Jacob forever, and of his kingdom there will be no end."

34 And Mary said to the angel, "How will this be, since I am a virgin?"

35 And the angel answered her, "The Holy Spirit will come upon you, and the power of the Most High will overshadow you; therefore the child to be born will be called holy—the Son of God. 36 And behold, your relative Elizabeth in her old age has also conceived a son, and this is the sixth month with her who was called barren. 37 For nothing will be impossible with God." 38 And Mary said, "Behold, I am the servant of the Lord; let it be to me according to your word." And the angel departed from her.

39 In those days Mary arose and went with haste into the hill country, to a town in Judah, 40 and she entered the house of Zechariah and greeted Elizabeth. 41 And when Elizabeth heard the greeting of Mary, the baby leaped in her womb. And Elizabeth was filled with the Holy Spirit, 42 and she exclaimed with a loud cry, "Blessed are you among women, and blessed is the fruit of your womb! 43 And why is this granted to me that the mother of my Lord should come to me? 44 For behold, when the sound of your greeting came to my ears, the baby in my womb leaped for joy. 45 And blessed is she who believed that there would be a fulfillment of what was spoken to her from the Lord."

Time of Reflection

What does God say in this passage that stands out to you?

What does it teach you about God and yourself?

How will you respond in faith and obedience today?

Prayer of Confession

Prayer of Supplication

Our government leaders

Weekly Collect

Merciful God, who sent Your messengers the prophets to preach repentance and prepare the way for our salvation: Give us grace to heed their warnings and forsake our sins, that we may greet with joy the coming of Jesus Christ our Redeemer; who lives and reigns with You and the Holy Spirit, one God, now and forever. *Amen.*

SATURDAY, DECEMBER 12

Call to Worship

> 21 My mouth will speak the praise of the LORD,
> and let all flesh bless his holy name forever and ever. (Psalm 145:21)

Prayers of Adoration and Thanksgiving

Psalm 9:1-2

> 1 I will give thanks to the LORD with my whole heart;
>   I will recount all of your wonderful deeds.
> 2 I will be glad and exult in you;
>   I will sing praise to your name, O Most High.

Scripture Reading: Luke 1:46-56

> 46 And Mary said,
> "My soul magnifies the Lord,
> 47 and my spirit rejoices in God my Savior,
> 48 for he has looked on the humble estate of his servant.
> For behold, from now on all generations will call me blessed;
> 49 for he who is mighty has done great things for me,
> and holy is his name.
> 50 And his mercy is for those who fear him
> from generation to generation.
> 51 He has shown strength with his arm;
> he has scattered the proud in the thoughts of their hearts;
> 52 he has brought down the mighty from their thrones
> and exalted those of humble estate;
> 53 he has filled the hungry with good things,
> and the rich he has sent away empty.
> 54 He has helped his servant Israel,
> in remembrance of his mercy,
> 55 as he spoke to our fathers,
> to Abraham and to his offspring forever."
> 56 And Mary remained with her about three months and returned to her home.

Time of Reflection

What does God say in this passage that stands out to you?

What does it teach you about God and yourself?

How will you respond in faith and obedience today?

Prayer of Confession

Prayer of Supplication
>Our first responders

Weekly Collect
>Merciful God, who sent Your messengers the prophets to preach repentance and prepare the way for our salvation: Give us grace to heed their warnings and forsake our sins, that we may greet with joy the coming of Jesus Christ our Redeemer; who lives and reigns with You and the Holy Spirit, one God, now and forever. *Amen.*

SUNDAY, DECEMBER 13

Psalm 92

> A Psalm. A Song for the Sabbath.
> 1 It is good to give thanks to the LORD,
>   to sing praises to your name, O Most High;
> 2 to declare your steadfast love in the morning,
>   and your faithfulness by night,
> 3 to the music of the lute and the harp,
>   to the melody of the lyre.
> 4 For you, O LORD, have made me glad by your work;
>   at the works of your hands I sing for joy.
> 5 How great are your works, O LORD!
>   Your thoughts are very deep!
> 6 The stupid man cannot know;
>   the fool cannot understand this:
> 7 that though the wicked sprout like grass
>   and all evildoers flourish,
> they are doomed to destruction forever;
> 8   but you, O LORD, are on high forever.
> 9 For behold, your enemies, O LORD,
>   for behold, your enemies shall perish;
>   all evildoers shall be scattered.
> 10 But you have exalted my horn like that of the wild ox;
>   you have poured over me fresh oil.
> 11 My eyes have seen the downfall of my enemies;
>   my ears have heard the doom of my evil assailants.
> 12 The righteous flourish like the palm tree
>   and grow like a cedar in Lebanon.
> 13 They are planted in the house of the LORD;
>   they flourish in the courts of our God.
> 14 They still bear fruit in old age;
>   they are ever full of sap and green,
> 15 to declare that the LORD is upright;
>   he is my rock, and there is no unrighteousness in him.

Sermon Notes

MONDAY, DECEMBER 14

Call to Worship

1 In the beginning was the Word, and the Word was with God, and the Word was God. (John 1:1)

Prayers of Adoration and Thanksgiving

Psalm 89:1-4

1 I will sing of the steadfast love of the LORD, forever;
　with my mouth I will make known your faithfulness to all generations.
2 For I said, "Steadfast love will be built up forever;
　in the heavens you will establish your faithfulness."
3 You have said, "I have made a covenant with my chosen one;
　I have sworn to David my servant:
4 'I will establish your offspring forever,
　and build your throne for all generations.'"

Scripture Reading: Luke 1:57-80

57 Now the time came for Elizabeth to give birth, and she bore a son. 58 And her neighbors and relatives heard that the Lord had shown great mercy to her, and they rejoiced with her. 59 And on the eighth day they came to circumcise the child. And they would have called him Zechariah after his father, 60 but his mother answered, "No; he shall be called John." 61 And they said to her, "None of your relatives is called by this name." 62 And they made signs to his father, inquiring what he wanted him to be called. 63 And he asked for a writing tablet and wrote, "His name is John." And they all wondered. 64 And immediately his mouth was opened and his tongue loosed, and he spoke, blessing God. 65 And fear came on all their neighbors. And all these things were talked about through all the hill country of Judea, 66 and all who heard them laid them up in their hearts, saying, "What then will this child be?" For the hand of the Lord was with him.
67 And his father Zechariah was filled with the Holy Spirit and prophesied, saying,
68 "Blessed be the Lord God of Israel,
for he has visited and redeemed his people
69 and has raised up a horn of salvation for us
in the house of his servant David,
70 as he spoke by the mouth of his holy prophets from of old,
71 that we should be saved from our enemies
and from the hand of all who hate us;
72 to show the mercy promised to our fathers
and to remember his holy covenant,
73 the oath that he swore to our father Abraham, to grant us
74 that we, being delivered from the hand of our enemies,

might serve him without fear,
75 in holiness and righteousness before him all our days.
76 And you, child, will be called the prophet of the Most High;
for you will go before the Lord to prepare his ways,
77 to give knowledge of salvation to his people
in the forgiveness of their sins,
78 because of the tender mercy of our God,
whereby the sunrise shall visit us from on high
79 to give light to those who sit in darkness and in the shadow of death,
to guide our feet into the way of peace."
80 And the child grew and became strong in spirit, and he was in the wilderness until the day of his public appearance to Israel.

Time of Reflection

What does God say in this passage that stands out to you?

What does it teach you about God and yourself?

How will you respond in faith and obedience today?

Prayer of Confession

Prayer of Supplication

All who are spiritually weary and seek rest

Weekly Collect

Stir up Your power, O Lord, and with great might come among us; and, because we are sorely hindered by our sins, let Your bountiful grace and mercy speedily help and deliver us; through Jesus Christ our Lord, to whom, with You and the Holy Spirit, be honor and glory, now and forever. *Amen.*

TUESDAY, DECEMBER 15

Call to Worship

15 He is the image of the invisible God, the firstborn of all creation. (Colossians 1:15)

Prayers of Adoration and Thanksgiving

Psalm 116:8-9

8 For you have delivered my soul from death,
 my eyes from tears,
 my feet from stumbling;
9 I will walk before the LORD
 in the land of the living

Scripture Reading: Revelation 21:1-8

1 Then I saw a new heaven and a new earth, for the first heaven and the first earth had passed away, and the sea was no more. 2 And I saw the holy city, new Jerusalem, coming down out of heaven from God, prepared as a bride adorned for her husband. 3 And I heard a loud voice from the throne saying, "Behold, the dwelling place of God is with man. He will dwell with them, and they will be his people, and God himself will be with them as their God. 4 He will wipe away every tear from their eyes, and death shall be no more, neither shall there be mourning, nor crying, nor pain anymore, for the former things have passed away."

5 And he who was seated on the throne said, "Behold, I am making all things new." Also he said, "Write this down, for these words are trustworthy and true." 6 And he said to me, "It is done! I am the Alpha and the Omega, the beginning and the end. To the thirsty I will give from the spring of the water of life without payment. 7 The one who conquers will have this heritage, and I will be his God and he will be my son. 8 But as for the cowardly, the faithless, the detestable, as for murderers, the sexually immoral, sorcerers, idolaters, and all liars, their portion will be in the lake that burns with fire and sulfur, which is the second death."

Time of Reflection

What does God say in this passage that stands out to you?

What does it teach you about God and yourself?

How will you respond in faith and obedience today?

Prayer of Confession

Prayer of Supplication

All who sin and need a Savior

Weekly Collect

Stir up Your power, O Lord, and with great might come among us; and, because we are sorely hindered by our sins, let Your bountiful grace and mercy speedily help and deliver us; through Jesus Christ our Lord, to whom, with You and the Holy Spirit, be honor and glory, now and forever. *Amen.*

WEDNESDAY, DECEMBER 16

Call to Worship

> 3 All things were made through him, and without him was not any thing made that was made. (John 1:3)

Prayers of Adoration and Thanksgiving

Psalm 66

> 1 Shout for joy to God, all the earth;
> 2   sing the glory of his name;
>   give to him glorious praise!
> 3 Say to God, "How awesome are your deeds!
>   So great is your power that your enemies come cringing to you.
> 4 All the earth worships you
>   and sings praises to you;
>   they sing praises to your name."

Scripture Reading: Revelation 21:9-27

> 9 Then came one of the seven angels who had the seven bowls full of the seven last plagues and spoke to me, saying, "Come, I will show you the Bride, the wife of the Lamb." 10 And he carried me away in the Spirit to a great, high mountain, and showed me the holy city Jerusalem coming down out of heaven from God, 11 having the glory of God, its radiance like a most rare jewel, like a jasper, clear as crystal. 12 It had a great, high wall, with twelve gates, and at the gates twelve angels, and on the gates the names of the twelve tribes of the sons of Israel were inscribed— 13 on the east three gates, on the north three gates, on the south three gates, and on the west three gates. 14 And the wall of the city had twelve foundations, and on them were the twelve names of the twelve apostles of the Lamb.

> 15 And the one who spoke with me had a measuring rod of gold to measure the city and its gates and walls. 16 The city lies foursquare, its length the same as its width. And he measured the city with his rod, 12,000 stadia. Its length and width and height are equal. 17 He also measured its wall, 144 cubits by human measurement, which is also an angel's measurement. 18 The wall was built of jasper, while the city was pure gold, like clear glass. 19 The foundations of the wall of the city were adorned with every kind of jewel. The first was jasper, the second sapphire, the third agate, the fourth emerald, 20 the fifth onyx, the sixth carnelian, the seventh chrysolite, the eighth beryl, the ninth topaz, the tenth chrysoprase, the eleventh jacinth, the twelfth amethyst. 21 And the twelve gates were twelve pearls, each of the gates made of a single pearl, and the street of the city was pure gold, like transparent glass.

22 And I saw no temple in the city, for its temple is the Lord God the Almighty and the Lamb. 23 And the city has no need of sun or moon to shine on it, for the glory of God gives it light, and its lamp is the Lamb. 24 By its light will the nations walk, and the kings of the earth will bring their glory into it, 25 and its gates will never be shut by day—and there will be no night there. 26 They will bring into it the glory and the honor of the nations. 27 But nothing unclean will ever enter it, nor anyone who does what is detestable or false, but only those who are written in the Lamb's book of life.

Time of Reflection

What does God say in this passage that stands out to you?

What does it teach you about God and yourself?

How will you respond in faith and obedience today?

Prayer of Confession

Prayer of Supplication

All who mourn and long for comfort

Weekly Collect

Stir up Your power, O Lord, and with great might come among us; and, because we are sorely hindered by our sins, let Your bountiful grace and mercy speedily help and deliver us; through Jesus Christ our Lord, to whom, with You and the Holy Spirit, be honor and glory, now and forever. *Amen.*

THURSDAY, DECEMBER 17

Call to Worship

16 For by him all things were created, in heaven and on earth, visible and invisible, whether thrones or dominions or rulers or authorities—all things were created through him and for him. (Colossians 1:16)

Prayers of Adoration and Thanksgiving

Psalm 46:4-9

4 There is a river whose streams make glad the city of God,
   the holy habitation of the Most High.
5 God is in the midst of her; she shall not be moved;
   God will help her when morning dawns.
6 The nations rage, the kingdoms totter;
   he utters his voice, the earth melts.
7 The LORD of hosts is with us;
   the God of Jacob is our fortress. Selah
8 Come, behold the works of the LORD,
   how he has brought desolations on the earth.
9 He makes wars cease to the end of the earth;
   he breaks the bow and shatters the spear;
   he burns the chariots with fire.

Scripture Reading: Micah 4:1-7

1 It shall come to pass in the latter days
that the mountain of the house of the Lord
shall be established as the highest of the mountains,
and it shall be lifted up above the hills;
and peoples shall flow to it,
2 and many nations shall come, and say:
"Come, let us go up to the mountain of the LORD,
to the house of the God of Jacob,
that he may teach us his ways
and that we may walk in his paths."
For out of Zion shall go forth the law,
and the word of the LORD from Jerusalem.
3 He shall judge between many peoples,
and shall decide disputes for strong nations far away;
and they shall beat their swords into plowshares,
and their spears into pruning hooks;
nation shall not lift up sword against nation,
neither shall they learn war anymore;
4 but they shall sit every man under his vine and under his fig tree,
and no one shall make them afraid,
for the mouth of the LORD of hosts has spoken.

5 For all the peoples walk
each in the name of its god,
but we will walk in the name of the LORD our God
forever and ever.
6 In that day, declares the LORD,
I will assemble the lame
and gather those who have been driven away
and those whom I have afflicted;
7 and the lame I will make the remnant,
and those who were cast off, a strong nation;
and the LORD will reign over them in Mount Zion
from this time forth and forevermore.

Time of Reflection

What does God say in this passage that stands out to you?

What does it teach you about God and yourself?

How will you respond in faith and obedience today?

Prayer of Confession

Prayer of Supplication

All who struggle and desire victory

Weekly Collect

Stir up Your power, O Lord, and with great might come among us; and, because we are sorely hindered by our sins, let Your bountiful grace and mercy speedily help and deliver us; through Jesus Christ our Lord, to whom, with You and the Holy Spirit, be honor and glory, now and forever. *Amen.*

FRIDAY, DECEMBER 18

Call to Worship

4 In him was life, and the life was the light of men. 5 The light shines in the darkness, and the darkness has not overcome it. (John 1:4-5)

Prayers of Adoration and Thanksgiving

Psalm 16:5-11

5 The LORD is my chosen portion and my cup;
   you hold my lot.
6 The lines have fallen for me in pleasant places;
   indeed, I have a beautiful inheritance.
7 I bless the LORD who gives me counsel;
   in the night also my heart instructs me.
8 I have set the LORD always before me;
   because he is at my right hand, I shall not be shaken.
9 Therefore my heart is glad, and my whole being rejoices;
   my flesh also dwells secure.
10 For you will not abandon my soul to Sheol,
   or let your holy one see corruption.
11 You make known to me the path of life;
   in your presence there is fullness of joy;
   at your right hand are pleasures forevermore.

Scripture Reading: Genesis 22:1-14, Hebrews 11:17-19

1 After these things God tested Abraham and said to him, "Abraham!" And he said, "Here I am." 2 He said, "Take your son, your only son Isaac, whom you love, and go to the land of Moriah, and offer him there as a burnt offering on one of the mountains of which I shall tell you." 3 So Abraham rose early in the morning, saddled his donkey, and took two of his young men with him, and his son Isaac. And he cut the wood for the burnt offering and arose and went to the place of which God had told him. 4 On the third day Abraham lifted up his eyes and saw the place from afar. 5 Then Abraham said to his young men, "Stay here with the donkey; I and the boy will go over there and worship and come again to you." 6 And Abraham took the wood of the burnt offering and laid it on Isaac his son. And he took in his hand the fire and the knife. So they went both of them together. 7 And Isaac said to his father Abraham, "My father!" And he said, "Here I am, my son." He said, "Behold, the fire and the wood, but where is the lamb for a burnt offering?" 8 Abraham said, "God will provide for himself the lamb for a burnt offering, my son." So they went both of them together.

9 When they came to the place of which God had told him, Abraham built the altar there and laid the wood in order and bound Isaac his son and laid him on the altar, on top of the wood. 10 Then Abraham reached

out his hand and took the knife to slaughter his son. 11 But the angel of the LORD called to him from heaven and said, "Abraham, Abraham!" And he said, "Here I am." 12 He said, "Do not lay your hand on the boy or do anything to him, for now I know that you fear God, seeing you have not withheld your son, your only son, from me." 13 And Abraham lifted up his eyes and looked, and behold, behind him was a ram, caught in a thicket by his horns. And Abraham went and took the ram and offered it up as a burnt offering instead of his son. 14 So Abraham called the name of that place, "The LORD will provide"; as it is said to this day, "On the mount of the LORD it shall be provided."

Hebrews 11:17-19

17 By faith Abraham, when he was tested, offered up Isaac, and he who had received the promises was in the act of offering up his only son, 18 of whom it was said, "Through Isaac shall your offspring be named." 19 He considered that God was able even to raise him from the dead, from which, figuratively speaking, he did receive him back.

Time of Reflection

What does God say in this passage that stands out to you?

What does it teach you about God and yourself?

How will you respond in faith and obedience today?

Prayer of Confession

Prayer of Supplication

All who are strangers and want fellowship

Weekly Collect

Stir up Your power, O Lord, and with great might come among us; and, because we are sorely hindered by our sins, let Your bountiful grace and mercy speedily help and deliver us; through Jesus Christ our Lord, to whom, with You and the Holy Spirit, be honor and glory, now and forever. *Amen.*

SATURDAY, DECEMBER 19

Call to Worship

17 And he is before all things, and in him all things hold together. (Colossians 1:17)

Prayers of Adoration and Thanksgiving

Psalm 89:1-4

1 I will sing of the steadfast love of the LORD, forever;
   with my mouth I will make known your faithfulness to all generations.
2 For I said, "Steadfast love will be built up forever;
   in the heavens you will establish your faithfulness."
3 You have said, "I have made a covenant with my chosen one;
   I have sworn to David my servant:
4 'I will establish your offspring forever,
   and build your throne for all generations.'"

Scripture Reading: Genesis 28:10-22

10 Jacob left Beersheba and went toward Haran. 11 And he came to a certain place and stayed there that night, because the sun had set. Taking one of the stones of the place, he put it under his head and lay down in that place to sleep. 12 And he dreamed, and behold, there was a ladder set up on the earth, and the top of it reached to heaven. And behold, the angels of God were ascending and descending on it! 13 And behold, the LORD stood above it and said, "I am the LORD, the God of Abraham your father and the God of Isaac. The land on which you lie I will give to you and to your offspring. 14 Your offspring shall be like the dust of the earth, and you shall spread abroad to the west and to the east and to the north and to the south, and in you and your offspring shall all the families of the earth be blessed. 15 Behold, I am with you and will keep you wherever you go, and will bring you back to this land. For I will not leave you until I have done what I have promised you." 16 Then Jacob awoke from his sleep and said, "Surely the LORD is in this place, and I did not know it." 17 And he was afraid and said, "How awesome is this place! This is none other than the house of God, and this is the gate of heaven."

18 So early in the morning Jacob took the stone that he had put under his head and set it up for a pillar and poured oil on the top of it. 19 He called the name of that place Bethel, but the name of the city was Luz at the first. 20 Then Jacob made a vow, saying, "If God will be with me and will keep me in this way that I go, and will give me bread to eat and clothing to wear, 21 so that I come again to my father's house in peace, then the LORD shall be my God, 22 and this stone, which I have set up for a pillar, shall be God's house. And of all that you give me I will give a full tenth to you."

Time of Reflection

    What does God say in this passage that stands out to you?

    What does it teach you about God and yourself?

    How will you respond in faith and obedience today?

Prayer of Confession

Prayer of Supplication

    All who hunger and thirst after righteousness

Weekly Collect

    Stir up Your power, O Lord, and with great might come among us; and, because we are sorely hindered by our sins, let Your bountiful grace and mercy speedily help and deliver us; through Jesus Christ our Lord, to whom, with You and the Holy Spirit, be honor and glory, now and forever. *Amen.*

SUNDAY, DECEMBER 20

Psalm 92

> A Psalm. A Song for the Sabbath.
> 1 It is good to give thanks to the LORD,
>   to sing praises to your name, O Most High;
> 2 to declare your steadfast love in the morning,
>   and your faithfulness by night,
> 3 to the music of the lute and the harp,
>   to the melody of the lyre.
> 4 For you, O LORD, have made me glad by your work;
>   at the works of your hands I sing for joy.
> 5 How great are your works, O LORD!
>   Your thoughts are very deep!
> 6 The stupid man cannot know;
>   the fool cannot understand this:
> 7 that though the wicked sprout like grass
>   and all evildoers flourish,
> they are doomed to destruction forever;
> 8   but you, O LORD, are on high forever.
> 9 For behold, your enemies, O LORD,
>   for behold, your enemies shall perish;
>   all evildoers shall be scattered.
> 10 But you have exalted my horn like that of the wild ox;
>   you have poured over me fresh oil.
> 11 My eyes have seen the downfall of my enemies;
>   my ears have heard the doom of my evil assailants.
> 12 The righteous flourish like the palm tree
>   and grow like a cedar in Lebanon.
> 13 They are planted in the house of the LORD;
>   they flourish in the courts of our God.
> 14 They still bear fruit in old age;
>   they are ever full of sap and green,
> 15 to declare that the LORD is upright;
>   he is my rock, and there is no unrighteousness in him.

Sermon Notes

MONDAY, DECEMBER 21

Call to Worship

18 And he is the head of the body, the church. He is the beginning, the firstborn from the dead, that in everything he might be preeminent. (Colossians 1:18)

Prayers of Adoration and Thanksgiving

Psalm 8:3-9

3 When I look at your heavens, the work of your fingers,
  the moon and the stars, which you have set in place,
4 what is man that you are mindful of him,
  and the son of man that you care for him?
Yet you have made him a little lower than the heavenly beings
  and crowned him with glory and honor.
6 You have given him dominion over the works of your hands;
  you have put all things under his feet,
7 all sheep and oxen,
  and also the beasts of the field,
8 the birds of the heavens, and the fish of the sea,
  whatever passes along the paths of the seas.
9 O LORD, our Lord,
  how majestic is your name in all the earth!

Scripture Reading: Philippians 2:5-11

5 Have this mind among yourselves, which is yours in Christ Jesus, 6 who, though he was in the form of God, did not count equality with God a thing to be grasped, 7 but emptied himself, by taking the form of a servant, being born in the likeness of men. 8 And being found in human form, he humbled himself by becoming obedient to the point of death, even death on a cross. 9 Therefore God has highly exalted him and bestowed on him the name that is above every name, 10 so that at the name of Jesus every knee should bow, in heaven and on earth and under the earth, 11 and every tongue confess that Jesus Christ is Lord, to the glory of God the Father.

Time of Reflection

What does God say in this passage that stands out to you?

What does it teach you about God and yourself?

How will you respond in faith and obedience today?

Prayer of Confession

Prayer of Supplication
How God may be calling each person to connect with new relationships

Weekly Collect
Purify our conscience, Almighty God, by Your daily visitation, that Your Son Jesus Christ, at His coming, may find in us a mansion prepared for Himself; who lives and reigns with You, in the unity of the Holy Spirit, one God, now and forever. *Amen.*

TUESDAY, DECEMBER 22

Call to Worship

19 For in him all the fullness of God was pleased to dwell, 20 and through him to reconcile to himself all things, whether on earth or in heaven, making peace by the blood of his cross. (Colossians 1:19-20)

Prayers of Adoration and Thanksgiving

Psalm 27:13-14

13 I believe that I shall look upon the goodness of the LORD
   in the land of the living!
14 Wait for the LORD;
   be strong, and let your heart take courage;
   wait for the LORD!

Scripture Reading: Titus 2:11 – 3:7

11 For the grace of God has appeared, bringing salvation for all people, 12 training us to renounce ungodliness and worldly passions, and to live self-controlled, upright, and godly lives in the present age, 13 waiting for our blessed hope, the appearing of the glory of our great God and Savior Jesus Christ, 14 who gave himself for us to redeem us from all lawlessness and to purify for himself a people for his own possession who are zealous for good works.

15 Declare these things; exhort and rebuke with all authority. Let no one disregard you.

1 Remind them to be submissive to rulers and authorities, to be obedient, to be ready for every good work, 2 to speak evil of no one, to avoid quarreling, to be gentle, and to show perfect courtesy toward all people. 3 For we ourselves were once foolish, disobedient, led astray, slaves to various passions and pleasures, passing our days in malice and envy, hated by others and hating one another. 4 But when the goodness and loving kindness of God our Savior appeared, 5 he saved us, not because of works done by us in righteousness, but according to his own mercy, by the washing of regeneration and renewal of the Holy Spirit, 6 whom he poured out on us richly through Jesus Christ our Savior, 7 so that being justified by his grace we might become heirs according to the hope of eternal life.

Time of Reflection

What does God say in this passage that stands out to you?

What does it teach you about God and yourself?

How will you respond in faith and obedience today?

Prayer of Confession

Prayer of Supplication

> The transforming presence of the Kingdom of our Lord Jesus Christ in Dallas and to the world

Weekly Collect

> Purify our conscience, Almighty God, by Your daily visitation, that Your Son Jesus Christ, at His coming, may find in us a mansion prepared for Himself; who lives and reigns with You, in the unity of the Holy Spirit, one God, now and forever. *Amen.*

WEDNESDAY, DECEMBER 23

Call to Worship

21 And you, who once were alienated and hostile in mind, doing evil deeds, 22 he has now reconciled in his body of flesh by his death, in order to present you holy and blameless and above reproach before him… (Colossians 1:21-22)

Prayers of Adoration and Thanksgiving

Psalm 89:20, 28-29

20 I have found David, my servant;
   with my holy oil I have anointed him,
28 My steadfast love I will keep for him forever,
   and my covenant will stand firm for him.
29 I will establish his offspring forever
   and his throne as the days of the heavens.

Scripture Reading: Matthew 1:1-17

1 The book of the genealogy of Jesus Christ, the son of David, the son of Abraham.

2 Abraham was the father of Isaac, and Isaac the father of Jacob, and Jacob the father of Judah and his brothers, 3 and Judah the father of Perez and Zerah by Tamar, and Perez the father of Hezron, and Hezron the father of Ram, 4 and Ram the father of Amminadab, and Amminadab the father of Nahshon, and Nahshon the father of Salmon, 5 and Salmon the father of Boaz by Rahab, and Boaz the father of Obed by Ruth, and Obed the father of Jesse, 6 and Jesse the father of David the king.

And David was the father of Solomon by the wife of Uriah, 7 and Solomon the father of Rehoboam, and Rehoboam the father of Abijah, and Abijah the father of Asaph, 8 and Asaph the father of Jehoshaphat, and Jehoshaphat the father of Joram, and Joram the father of Uzziah, 9 and Uzziah the father of Jotham, and Jotham the father of Ahaz, and Ahaz the father of Hezekiah, 10 and Hezekiah the father of Manasseh, and Manasseh the father of Amos, and Amos the father of Josiah, 11 and Josiah the father of Jechoniah and his brothers, at the time of the deportation to Babylon.

12 And after the deportation to Babylon: Jechoniah was the father of Shealtiel, and Shealtiel the father of Zerubbabel, 13 and Zerubbabel the father of Abiud, and Abiud the father of Eliakim, and Eliakim the father of Azor, 14 and Azor the father of Zadok, and Zadok the father of Achim, and Achim the father of Eliud, 15 and Eliud the father of Eleazar, and Eleazar the father of Matthan, and Matthan the father of Jacob, 16 and Jacob the father of Joseph the husband of Mary, of whom Jesus was born, who is called Christ.

17 So all the generations from Abraham to David were fourteen generations, and from David to the deportation to Babylon fourteen generations, and from the deportation to Babylon to the Christ fourteen generations.

Time of Reflection

What does God say in this passage that stands out to you?

What does it teach you about God and yourself?

How will you respond in faith and obedience today?

Prayer of Confession

Prayer of Supplication

PCPC's witness to employees in businesses near the church

Weekly Collect

Purify our conscience, Almighty God, by Your daily visitation, that Your Son Jesus Christ, at His coming, may find in us a mansion prepared for Himself; who lives and reigns with You, in the unity of the Holy Spirit, one God, now and forever. *Amen.*

THURSDAY, DECEMBER 24

Call to Worship

11 He came to his own, and his own people did not receive him. 12 But to all who did receive him, who believed in his name, he gave the right to become children of God… (John 1:11-12)

Prayers of Adoration and Thanksgiving

Psalm 27:1

The LORD is my light and my salvation;
  whom shall I fear?
The LORD is the stronghold of my life;
  of whom shall I be afraid?

Scripture Reading: Matthew 1:18-25

18 Now the birth of Jesus Christ took place in this way. When his mother Mary had been betrothed to Joseph, before they came together she was found to be with child from the Holy Spirit. 19 And her husband Joseph, being a just man and unwilling to put her to shame, resolved to divorce her quietly. 20 But as he considered these things, behold, an angel of the Lord appeared to him in a dream, saying, "Joseph, son of David, do not fear to take Mary as your wife, for that which is conceived in her is from the Holy Spirit. 21 She will bear a son, and you shall call his name Jesus, for he will save his people from their sins." 22 All this took place to fulfill what the Lord had spoken by the prophet:

23 "Behold, the virgin shall conceive and bear a son,

and they shall call his name Immanuel"

(which means, God with us). 24 When Joseph woke from sleep, he did as the angel of the Lord commanded him: he took his wife, 25 but knew her not until she had given birth to a son. And he called his name Jesus.

Time of Reflection

What does God say in this passage that stands out to you?

What does it teach you about God and yourself?

How will you respond in faith and obedience today?

Prayer of Confession

Prayer of Supplication

For our Sunday Morning Communities and Small Groups as they discover and meet needs in their communities

Weekly Collect

Purify our conscience, Almighty God, by Your daily visitation, that Your Son Jesus Christ, at His coming, may find in us a mansion prepared for Himself; who lives and reigns with You, in the unity of the Holy Spirit, one God, now and forever. *Amen.*

FRIDAY, DECEMBER 25

Call to Worship

14 And the Word became flesh and dwelt among us, and we have seen his glory, glory as of the only Son from the Father, full of grace and truth. (John 1:14)

Prayers of Adoration and Thanksgiving

Psalm 8:1-2

1 O LORD, our Lord,
　how majestic is your name in all the earth!
You have set your glory above the heavens.
2　Out of the mouth of babies and infants,
you have established strength because of your foes,
　to still the enemy and the avenger.

Scripture Reading: Luke 2:1-21

1 In those days a decree went out from Caesar Augustus that all the world should be registered. 2 This was the first registration when Quirinius was governor of Syria. 3 And all went to be registered, each to his own town. 4 And Joseph also went up from Galilee, from the town of Nazareth, to Judea, to the city of David, which is called Bethlehem, because he was of the house and lineage of David, 5 to be registered with Mary, his betrothed, who was with child. 6 And while they were there, the time came for her to give birth. 7 And she gave birth to her firstborn son and wrapped him in swaddling cloths and laid him in a manger, because there was no place for them in the inn.

8 And in the same region there were shepherds out in the field, keeping watch over their flock by night. 9 And an angel of the Lord appeared to them, and the glory of the Lord shone around them, and they were filled with great fear. 10 And the angel said to them, "Fear not, for behold, I bring you good news of great joy that will be for all the people. 11 For unto you is born this day in the city of David a Savior, who is Christ the Lord. 12 And this will be a sign for you: you will find a baby wrapped in swaddling cloths and lying in a manger." 13 And suddenly there was with the angel a multitude of the heavenly host praising God and saying,

14 "Glory to God in the highest,

and on earth peace among those with whom he is pleased!"

15 When the angels went away from them into heaven, the shepherds said to one another, "Let us go over to Bethlehem and see this thing that has happened, which the Lord has made known to us." 16 And they went with haste and found Mary and Joseph, and the baby lying in a manger. 17 And when they saw it, they made known the saying that had been told them concerning this child. 18 And all who heard it wondered at

what the shepherds told them. 19 But Mary treasured up all these things, pondering them in her heart. 20 And the shepherds returned, glorifying and praising God for all they had heard and seen, as it had been told them.

21 And at the end of eight days, when he was circumcised, he was called Jesus, the name given by the angel before he was conceived in the womb.

Time of Reflection

What does God say in this passage that stands out to you?

What does it teach you about God and yourself?

How will you respond in faith and obedience today?

Prayer of Confession

Prayer of Supplication

PCPC's reach to unchurched families in our city

Weekly Collect

O God, You have caused this holy night to shine with the brightness of the true Light: Grant that we, who have known the mystery of that Light on earth, may also enjoy Him perfectly in heaven; where with You and the Holy Spirit He lives and reigns, one God, in glory everlasting. *Amen.*

SATURDAY, DECEMBER 26

Call to Worship

16 For from his fullness we have all received, grace upon grace. (John 1:16)

Prayers of Adoration and Thanksgiving

Psalm 116:5-7

5 Gracious is the LORD, and righteous;
   our God is merciful.
6 The LORD preserves the simple;
   when I was brought low, he saved me.
7 Return, O my soul, to your rest;
   for the LORD has dealt bountifully with you.

Scripture Reading: Luke 2:22-38

22 And when the time came for their purification according to the Law of Moses, they brought him up to Jerusalem to present him to the Lord 23 (as it is written in the Law of the Lord, "Every male who first opens the womb shall be called holy to the Lord") 24 and to offer a sacrifice according to what is said in the Law of the Lord, "a pair of turtledoves, or two young pigeons." 25 Now there was a man in Jerusalem, whose name was Simeon, and this man was righteous and devout, waiting for the consolation of Israel, and the Holy Spirit was upon him. 26 And it had been revealed to him by the Holy Spirit that he would not see death before he had seen the Lord's Christ. 27 And he came in the Spirit into the temple, and when the parents brought in the child Jesus, to do for him according to the custom of the Law, 28 he took him up in his arms and blessed God and said,

29 "Lord, now you are letting your servant depart in peace,

according to your word;

30 for my eyes have seen your salvation

31 that you have prepared in the presence of all peoples,

32 a light for revelation to the Gentiles,

and for glory to your people Israel."

33 And his father and his mother marveled at what was said about him. 34 And Simeon blessed them and said to Mary his mother, "Behold, this child is appointed for the fall and rising of many in Israel, and for a sign that is opposed 35 (and a sword will pierce through your own soul also), so that thoughts from many hearts may be revealed."

36 And there was a prophetess, Anna, the daughter of Phanuel, of the tribe of Asher. She was advanced in years, having lived with her husband

seven years from when she was a virgin, 37 and then as a widow until she was eighty-four. She did not depart from the temple, worshiping with fasting and prayer night and day. 38 And coming up at that very hour she began to give thanks to God and to speak of him to all who were waiting for the redemption of Jerusalem.

Time of Reflection

What does God say in this passage that stands out to you?

What does it teach you about God and yourself?

How will you respond in faith and obedience today?

Prayer of Confession

Prayer of Supplication

For all who will come, that we would be a church who opens wide her doors and offers welcome in the name of the Lord Jesus Christ

Weekly Collect

Purify our conscience, Almighty God, by Your daily visitation, that Your Son Jesus Christ, at His coming, may find in us a mansion prepared for Himself; who lives and reigns with You, in the unity of the Holy Spirit, one God, now and forever. *Amen.*

SUNDAY, DECEMBER 27

Psalm 92

> A Psalm. A Song for the Sabbath.
> 1 It is good to give thanks to the LORD,
>   to sing praises to your name, O Most High;
> 2 to declare your steadfast love in the morning,
>   and your faithfulness by night,
> 3 to the music of the lute and the harp,
>   to the melody of the lyre.
> 4 For you, O LORD, have made me glad by your work;
>   at the works of your hands I sing for joy.
> 5 How great are your works, O LORD!
>   Your thoughts are very deep!
> 6 The stupid man cannot know;
>   the fool cannot understand this:
> 7 that though the wicked sprout like grass
>   and all evildoers flourish,
> they are doomed to destruction forever;
> 8   but you, O LORD, are on high forever.
> 9 For behold, your enemies, O LORD,
>   for behold, your enemies shall perish;
>   all evildoers shall be scattered.
> 10 But you have exalted my horn like that of the wild ox;
>   you have poured over me fresh oil.
> 11 My eyes have seen the downfall of my enemies;
>   my ears have heard the doom of my evil assailants.
> 12 The righteous flourish like the palm tree
>   and grow like a cedar in Lebanon.
> 13 They are planted in the house of the LORD;
>   they flourish in the courts of our God.
> 14 They still bear fruit in old age;
>   they are ever full of sap and green,
> 15 to declare that the LORD is upright;
>   he is my rock, and there is no unrighteousness in him.

Sermon Notes

MONDAY, DECEMBER 28

Call to Worship

> 1 Praise the LORD!
> Praise the LORD, O my soul!
> 2 I will praise the LORD as long as I live;
> I will sing praises to my God while I have my being.
> (Psalm 146:1-2)

Prayers of Adoration and Thanksgiving

Psalm 27:4

> 4 One thing have I asked of the LORD,
>   that will I seek after:
> that I may dwell in the house of the LORD
>   all the days of my life,
> to gaze upon the beauty of the LORD
>   and to inquire in his temple.

Scripture Reading: Luke 2:39-52

39 And when they had performed everything according to the Law of the Lord, they returned into Galilee, to their own town of Nazareth. 40 And the child grew and became strong, filled with wisdom. And the favor of God was upon him.

41 Now his parents went to Jerusalem every year at the Feast of the Passover. 42 And when he was twelve years old, they went up according to custom. 43 And when the feast was ended, as they were returning, the boy Jesus stayed behind in Jerusalem. His parents did not know it, 44 but supposing him to be in the group they went a day's journey, but then they began to search for him among their relatives and acquaintances, 45 and when they did not find him, they returned to Jerusalem, searching for him. 46 After three days they found him in the temple, sitting among the teachers, listening to them and asking them questions. 47 And all who heard him were amazed at his understanding and his answers. 48 And when his parents saw him, they were astonished. And his mother said to him, "Son, why have you treated us so? Behold, your father and I have been searching for you in great distress." 49 And he said to them, "Why were you looking for me? Did you not know that I must be in my Father's house?" 50 And they did not understand the saying that he spoke to them. 51 And he went down with them and came to Nazareth and was submissive to them. And his mother treasured up all these things in her heart.

52 And Jesus increased in wisdom and in stature and in favor with God and man.

Time of Reflection

> What does God say in this passage that stands out to you?
>
> What does it teach you about God and yourself?
>
> How will you respond in faith and obedience today?

Prayer of Confession

Prayer of Supplication

> For new adult baptisms and professions of faith this year

Weekly Collect

> Almighty God, You have poured upon us the new light of Your incarnate Word: Grant that this light, enkindled in our hearts, may shine forth in our lives; through Jesus Christ our Lord, who lives and reigns with You, in the unity of the Holy Spirit, one God, now and forever. *Amen.*

TUESDAY, DECEMBER 29

Call to Worship

> 7 Sing to the LORD with thanksgiving;
> make melody to our God on the lyre!
> (Psalm 147:7

Prayers of Adoration and Thanksgiving

Psalm 27:11-14

> 11 Teach me your way, O LORD,
> and lead me on a level path
> because of my enemies.
> 12 Give me not up to the will of my adversaries;
> for false witnesses have risen against me,
> and they breathe out violence.
> 13 I believe that I shall look upon the goodness of the LORD
> in the land of the living!
> 14 Wait for the LORD;
> be strong, and let your heart take courage;
> wait for the LORD!

Scripture Reading: Matthew 2:1-23

> 1 Now after Jesus was born in Bethlehem of Judea in the days of Herod the king, behold, wise men from the east came to Jerusalem, 2 saying, "Where is he who has been born king of the Jews? For we saw his star when it rose and have come to worship him." 3 When Herod the king heard this, he was troubled, and all Jerusalem with him; 4 and assembling all the chief priests and scribes of the people, he inquired of them where the Christ was to be born. 5 They told him, "In Bethlehem of Judea, for so it is written by the prophet:

> 6 "'And you, O Bethlehem, in the land of Judah,
> are by no means least among the rulers of Judah;
> for from you shall come a ruler
> who will shepherd my people Israel.'"

> 7 Then Herod summoned the wise men secretly and ascertained from them what time the star had appeared. 8 And he sent them to Bethlehem, saying, "Go and search diligently for the child, and when you have found him, bring me word, that I too may come and worship him." 9 After listening to the king, they went on their way. And behold, the star that they had seen when it rose went before them until it came to rest over the place where the child was. 10 When they saw the star, they rejoiced exceedingly with great joy. 11 And going into the house, they saw the child with Mary his mother, and they fell down and worshiped him. Then, opening their treasures, they offered him gifts, gold and frankincense and myrrh. 12 And being warned in a dream not to return to

Herod, they departed to their own country by another way.

13 Now when they had departed, behold, an angel of the Lord appeared to Joseph in a dream and said, "Rise, take the child and his mother, and flee to Egypt, and remain there until I tell you, for Herod is about to search for the child, to destroy him." 14 And he rose and took the child and his mother by night and departed to Egypt 15 and remained there until the death of Herod. This was to fulfill what the Lord had spoken by the prophet, "Out of Egypt I called my son."

16 Then Herod, when he saw that he had been tricked by the wise men, became furious, and he sent and killed all the male children in Bethlehem and in all that region who were two years old or under, according to the time that he had ascertained from the wise men. 17 Then was fulfilled what was spoken by the prophet Jeremiah:

18 "A voice was heard in Ramah,
weeping and loud lamentation,
Rachel weeping for her children;
she refused to be comforted, because they are no more."

19 But when Herod died, behold, an angel of the Lord appeared in a dream to Joseph in Egypt, 20 saying, "Rise, take the child and his mother and go to the land of Israel, for those who sought the child's life are dead." 21 And he rose and took the child and his mother and went to the land of Israel. 22 But when he heard that Archelaus was reigning over Judea in place of his father Herod, he was afraid to go there, and being warned in a dream he withdrew to the district of Galilee. 23 And he went and lived in a city called Nazareth, so that what was spoken by the prophets might be fulfilled, that he would be called a Nazarene.

Time of Reflection

What does God say in this passage that stands out to you?

What does it teach you about God and yourself?

How will you respond in faith and obedience today?

Prayer of Confession

Prayer of Supplication

For a spirit of hospitality in our church and in our everyday lives

Weekly Collect

Almighty God, You have poured upon us the new light of Your incarnate Word: Grant that this light, enkindled in our hearts, may shine forth in our lives; through Jesus Christ our Lord, who lives and reigns with You, in the unity of the Holy Spirit, one God, now and forever. *Amen.*

WEDNESDAY, DECEMBER 30

Call to Worship

1 Praise the LORD!
Praise the LORD from the heavens;
praise him in the heights!
2 Praise him, all his angels;
praise him, all his hosts!
(Psalm 148:1-2)

Prayers of Adoration and Thanksgiving

Psalm 119:105

105 Your word is a lamp to my feet
and a light to my path.

Scripture Reading: John 1:1-18

1 In the beginning was the Word, and the Word was with God, and the Word was God. 2 He was in the beginning with God. 3 All things were made through him, and without him was not any thing made that was made. 4 In him was life, and the life was the light of men. 5 The light shines in the darkness, and the darkness has not overcome it.

6 There was a man sent from God, whose name was John. 7 He came as a witness, to bear witness about the light, that all might believe through him. 8 He was not the light, but came to bear witness about the light.

9 The true light, which gives light to everyone, was coming into the world. 10 He was in the world, and the world was made through him, yet the world did not know him. 11 He came to his own, and his own people did not receive him. 12 But to all who did receive him, who believed in his name, he gave the right to become children of God, 13 who were born, not of blood nor of the will of the flesh nor of the will of man, but of God.

14 And the Word became flesh and dwelt among us, and we have seen his glory, glory as of the only Son from the Father, full of grace and truth. 15 (John bore witness about him, and cried out, "This was he of whom I said, 'He who comes after me ranks before me, because he was before me.'") 16 For from his fullness we have all received, grace upon grace. 17 For the law was given through Moses; grace and truth came through Jesus Christ. 18 No one has ever seen God; the only God, who is at the Father's side, he has made him known.

Time of Reflection

What does God say in this passage that stands out to you?

What does it teach you about God and yourself?

How will you respond in faith and obedience today?

Prayer of Confession

Prayer of Supplication

For a spirit of generosity in time, talents, and treasure

Weekly Collect

Almighty God, You have poured upon us the new light of Your incarnate Word: Grant that this light, enkindled in our hearts, may shine forth in our lives; through Jesus Christ our Lord, who lives and reigns with You, in the unity of the Holy Spirit, one God, now and forever. *Amen.*

THURSDAY, DECEMBER 31

Call to Worship

> 3 Praise him, sun and moon,
> praise him, all you shining stars!
> 4 Praise him, you highest heavens,
> and you waters above the heavens!
> (Psalm 148:3-4)

Prayers of Adoration and Thanksgiving

Psalm 110:1-4

> 1 The LORD says to my Lord:
>   "Sit at my right hand,
> until I make your enemies your footstool."
> 2 The LORD sends forth from Zion
>   your mighty scepter.
>   Rule in the midst of your enemies!
> 3 Your people will offer themselves freely
>   on the day of your power,
>   in holy garments;
> from the womb of the morning,
>   the dew of your youth will be yours.
> 4 The LORD has sworn
>   and will not change his mind,
> "You are a priest forever
>   after the order of Melchizedek."

Scripture Reading: John 1:19-36

> 19 And this is the testimony of John, when the Jews sent priests and Levites from Jerusalem to ask him, "Who are you?" 20 He confessed, and did not deny, but confessed, "I am not the Christ." 21 And they asked him, "What then? Are you Elijah?" He said, "I am not." "Are you the Prophet?" And he answered, "No." 22 So they said to him, "Who are you? We need to give an answer to those who sent us. What do you say about yourself?" 23 He said, "I am the voice of one crying out in the wilderness, 'Make straight the way of the Lord,' as the prophet Isaiah said."
>
> 24 (Now they had been sent from the Pharisees.) 25 They asked him, "Then why are you baptizing, if you are neither the Christ, nor Elijah, nor the Prophet?" 26 John answered them, "I baptize with water, but among you stands one you do not know, 27 even he who comes after me, the strap of whose sandal I am not worthy to untie." 28 These things took place in Bethany across the Jordan, where John was baptizing.
>
> 29 The next day he saw Jesus coming toward him, and said, "Behold, the Lamb of God, who takes away the sin of the world! 30 This is he of whom I said, 'After me comes a man who ranks before me, because he

was before me.' 31 I myself did not know him, but for this purpose I came baptizing with water, that he might be revealed to Israel." 32 And John bore witness: "I saw the Spirit descend from heaven like a dove, and it remained on him. 33 I myself did not know him, but he who sent me to baptize with water said to me, 'He on whom you see the Spirit descend and remain, this is he who baptizes with the Holy Spirit.' 34 And I have seen and have borne witness that this is the Son of God."

35 The next day again John was standing with two of his disciples, 36 and he looked at Jesus as he walked by and said, "Behold, the Lamb of God!"

Time of Reflection

What does God say in this passage that stands out to you?

What does it teach you about God and yourself?

How will you respond in faith and obedience today?

Prayer of Confession

Prayer of Supplication

EXTEND: New Doors

Weekly Collect

Almighty God, You have poured upon us the new light of Your incarnate Word: Grant that this light, enkindled in our hearts, may shine forth in our lives; through Jesus Christ our Lord, who lives and reigns with You, in the unity of the Holy Spirit, one God, now and forever. *Amen.*

FRIDAY, JANUARY 1

Call to Worship

> 5 Let them praise the name of the LORD!
> For he commanded and they were created.
> 6 And he established them forever and ever;
> he gave a decree, and it shall not pass away.
> (Psalm 148:5-6)

Prayers of Adoration and Thanksgiving

Psalm 110:5-7

> 5 The LORD is at your right hand;
>   he will shatter kings on the day of his wrath.
> 6 He will execute judgment among the nations,
>   filling them with corpses;
> he will shatter chiefs
>   over the wide earth.
> 7 He will drink from the brook by the way;
>   therefore he will lift up his head

Scripture Reading: Revelation 5:1-14

> 1 Then I saw in the right hand of him who was seated on the throne a scroll written within and on the back, sealed with seven seals. 2 And I saw a mighty angel proclaiming with a loud voice, "Who is worthy to open the scroll and break its seals?" 3 And no one in heaven or on earth or under the earth was able to open the scroll or to look into it, 4 and I began to weep loudly because no one was found worthy to open the scroll or to look into it. 5 And one of the elders said to me, "Weep no more; behold, the Lion of the tribe of Judah, the Root of David, has conquered, so that he can open the scroll and its seven seals."
>
> 6 And between the throne and the four living creatures and among the elders I saw a Lamb standing, as though it had been slain, with seven horns and with seven eyes, which are the seven spirits of God sent out into all the earth. 7 And he went and took the scroll from the right hand of him who was seated on the throne. 8 And when he had taken the scroll, the four living creatures and the twenty-four elders fell down before the Lamb, each holding a harp, and golden bowls full of incense, which are the prayers of the saints. 9 And they sang a new song, saying,
>
> "Worthy are you to take the scroll and to open its seals,
> for you were slain, and by your blood you ransomed people for God
> from every tribe and language and people and nation,
> 10 and you have made them a kingdom and priests to our God,
> and they shall reign on the earth."

11 Then I looked, and I heard around the throne and the living creatures and the elders the voice of many angels, numbering myriads of myriads and thousands of thousands, 12 saying with a loud voice,
"Worthy is the Lamb who was slain,
to receive power and wealth and wisdom and might
and honor and glory and blessing!"
13 And I heard every creature in heaven and on earth and under the earth and in the sea, and all that is in them, saying,
"To him who sits on the throne and to the Lamb
be blessing and honor and glory and might forever and ever!"
14 And the four living creatures said, "Amen!" and the elders fell down and worshiped.

Time of Reflection

What does God say in this passage that stands out to you?

What does it teach you about God and yourself?

How will you respond in faith and obedience today?

Prayer of Confession

Prayer of Supplication

EXTEND: New Churches

Weekly Collect

Eternal Father, You gave to Your incarnate Son the holy name of Jesus to be the sign of our salvation: Plant in every heart, we pray, the love of Him who is the Savior of the world, our Lord Jesus Christ; who lives and reigns with You and the Holy Spirit, one God, in glory everlasting. *Amen.*

SATURDAY, JANUARY 2

Call to Worship

7 Praise the LORD from the earth,
you great sea creatures and all deeps,
8 fire and hail, snow and mist,
stormy wind fulfilling his word!
(Psalm 148:7-8)

Prayers of Adoration and Thanksgiving

Psalm 130

1 Out of the depths I cry to you, O LORD!
2   O LORD, hear my voice!
Let your ears be attentive
   to the voice of my pleas for mercy!
3 If you, O LORD, should mark iniquities,
   O LORD, who could stand?
4 But with you there is forgiveness,
   that you may be feared.
5 I wait for the LORD, my soul waits,
   and in his word I hope;
6 my soul waits for the LORD
   more than watchmen for the morning,
   more than watchmen for the morning.
7 O Israel, hope in the LORD!
   For with the Lord there is steadfast love,
   and with him is plentiful redemption.
8 And he will redeem Israel
   from all his iniquities.

Scripture Reading: Matthew 25:1-13

1 "Then the kingdom of heaven will be like ten virgins who took their lamps and went to meet the bridegroom. 2 Five of them were foolish, and five were wise. 3 For when the foolish took their lamps, they took no oil with them, 4 but the wise took flasks of oil with their lamps. 5 As the bridegroom was delayed, they all became drowsy and slept. 6 But at midnight there was a cry, 'Here is the bridegroom! Come out to meet him.' 7 Then all those virgins rose and trimmed their lamps. 8 And the foolish said to the wise, 'Give us some of your oil, for our lamps are going out.' 9 But the wise answered, saying, 'Since there will not be enough for us and for you, go rather to the dealers and buy for yourselves.' 10 And while they were going to buy, the bridegroom came, and those who were ready went in with him to the marriage feast, and the door was shut. 11 Afterward the other virgins came also, saying, 'Lord, lord, open to us.' 12 But he answered, 'Truly, I say to you, I do not know you.' 13 Watch therefore, for you know neither the day nor the hour.

Time of Reflection

    What does God say in this passage that stands out to you?

    What does it teach you about God and yourself?

    How will you respond in faith and obedience today?

Prayer of Confession

Prayer of Supplication

    EXTEND: New City

Weekly Collect

    Eternal Father, You gave to Your incarnate Son the holy name of Jesus to be the sign of our salvation: Plant in every heart, we pray, the love of Him who is the Savior of the world, our Lord Jesus Christ; who lives and reigns with You and the Holy Spirit, one God, in glory everlasting. *Amen.*

SUNDAY, JANUARY 3

Psalm 92

A Psalm. A Song for the Sabbath.
1 It is good to give thanks to the LORD,
 to sing praises to your name, O Most High;
2 to declare your steadfast love in the morning,
 and your faithfulness by night,
3 to the music of the lute and the harp,
 to the melody of the lyre.
4 For you, O LORD, have made me glad by your work;
 at the works of your hands I sing for joy.
5 How great are your works, O LORD!
 Your thoughts are very deep!
6 The stupid man cannot know;
 the fool cannot understand this:
7 that though the wicked sprout like grass
 and all evildoers flourish,
they are doomed to destruction forever;
8   but you, O LORD, are on high forever.
9 For behold, your enemies, O LORD,
 for behold, your enemies shall perish;
 all evildoers shall be scattered.
10 But you have exalted my horn like that of the wild ox;
 you have poured over me fresh oil.
11 My eyes have seen the downfall of my enemies;
 my ears have heard the doom of my evil assailants.
12 The righteous flourish like the palm tree
 and grow like a cedar in Lebanon.
13 They are planted in the house of the LORD;
 they flourish in the courts of our God.
14 They still bear fruit in old age;
 they are ever full of sap and green,
15 to declare that the LORD is upright;
 he is my rock, and there is no unrighteousness in him.

Sermon Notes

MONDAY, JANUARY 4

Call to Worship

> 8 My mouth is filled with your praise,
>   and with your glory all the day.
> (Psalm 71:8)

Prayers of Adoration and Thanksgiving

Psalm 90:12-17

> 12 So teach us to number our days
>   that we may get a heart of wisdom.
> 13 Return, O LORD! How long?
>   Have pity on your servants!
> 14 Satisfy us in the morning with your steadfast love,
>   that we may rejoice and be glad all our days.
> 15 Make us glad for as many days as you have afflicted us,
>   and for as many years as we have seen evil.
> 16 Let your work be shown to your servants,
>   and your glorious power to their children.
> 17 Let the favor of the Lord our God be upon us,
>   and establish the work of our hands upon us;
>   yes, establish the work of our hands!

Scripture Reading: Matthew 25:14-30

> 14 "For it will be like a man going on a journey, who called his servants and entrusted to them his property. 15 To one he gave five talents, to another two, to another one, to each according to his ability. Then he went away. 16 He who had received the five talents went at once and traded with them, and he made five talents more. 17 So also he who had the two talents made two talents more. 18 But he who had received the one talent went and dug in the ground and hid his master's money.
> 19 Now after a long time the master of those servants came and settled accounts with them. 20 And he who had received the five talents came forward, bringing five talents more, saying, 'Master, you delivered to me five talents; here, I have made five talents more.' 21 His master said to him, 'Well done, good and faithful servant. You have been faithful over a little; I will set you over much. Enter into the joy of your master.'
> 22 And he also who had the two talents came forward, saying, 'Master, you delivered to me two talents; here, I have made two talents more.' 23 His master said to him, 'Well done, good and faithful servant. You have been faithful over a little; I will set you over much. Enter into the joy of your master.' 24 He also who had received the one talent came forward, saying, 'Master, I knew you to be a hard man, reaping where you did not sow, and gathering where you scattered no seed, 25 so I was afraid, and I went and hid your talent in the ground. Here, you have what is yours.'

26 But his master answered him, 'You wicked and slothful servant! You knew that I reap where I have not sown and gather where I scattered no seed? 27 Then you ought to have invested my money with the bankers, and at my coming I should have received what was my own with interest. 28 So take the talent from him and give it to him who has the ten talents. 29 For to everyone who has will more be given, and he will have an abundance. But from the one who has not, even what he has will be taken away. 30 And cast the worthless servant into the outer darkness. In that place there will be weeping and gnashing of teeth.'

Time of Reflection

What does God say in this passage that stands out to you?

What does it teach you about God and yourself?

How will you respond in faith and obedience today?

Prayer of Confession

Prayer of Supplication

PCPC connecting people to Christ and His Church

Weekly Collect

O God, who wonderfully created, and yet more wonderfully restored, the dignity of human nature: Grant that we may share the divine life of Him who humbled Himself to share our humanity, Your Son Jesus Christ; who lives and reigns with You, in the unity of the Holy Spirit, one God, for ever and ever. *Amen.*

TUESDAY, JANUARY 5

Call to Worship

> 7 How precious is your steadfast love, O God!
>   The children of mankind take refuge in the shadow of your wings.
> 9 For with you is the fountain of life;
>   in your light do we see light.
> (Psalm 36:7, 9)

Prayers of Adoration and Thanksgiving

Psalm 107:8-9

> 8 Let them thank the LORD for his steadfast love,
>   for his wondrous works to the children of man!
> 9 For he satisfies the longing soul,
>   and the hungry soul he fills with good things.

Scripture Reading: Matthew 25:31-46

31 "When the Son of Man comes in his glory, and all the angels with him, then he will sit on his glorious throne. 32 Before him will be gathered all the nations, and he will separate people one from another as a shepherd separates the sheep from the goats. 33 And he will place the sheep on his right, but the goats on the left. 34 Then the King will say to those on his right, 'Come, you who are blessed by my Father, inherit the kingdom prepared for you from the foundation of the world. 35 For I was hungry and you gave me food, I was thirsty and you gave me drink, I was a stranger and you welcomed me, 36 I was naked and you clothed me, I was sick and you visited me, I was in prison and you came to me.' 37 Then the righteous will answer him, saying, 'Lord, when did we see you hungry and feed you, or thirsty and give you drink? 38 And when did we see you a stranger and welcome you, or naked and clothe you? 39 And when did we see you sick or in prison and visit you?' 40 And the King will answer them, 'Truly, I say to you, as you did it to one of the least of these my brothers, you did it to me.'

41 "Then he will say to those on his left, 'Depart from me, you cursed, into the eternal fire prepared for the devil and his angels. 42 For I was hungry and you gave me no food, I was thirsty and you gave me no drink, 43 I was a stranger and you did not welcome me, naked and you did not clothe me, sick and in prison and you did not visit me.' 44 Then they also will answer, saying, 'Lord, when did we see you hungry or thirsty or a stranger or naked or sick or in prison, and did not minister to you?' 45 Then he will answer them, saying, 'Truly, I say to you, as you did not do it to one of the least of these, you did not do it to me.' 46 And these will go away into eternal punishment, but the righteous into eternal life."

Time of Reflection

What does God say in this passage that stands out to you?

What does it teach you about God and yourself?

How will you respond in faith and obedience today?

Prayer of Confession

Prayer of Supplication

Unity in the body at PCPC

Weekly Collect

O God, who wonderfully created, and yet more wonderfully restored, the dignity of human nature: Grant that we may share the divine life of Him who humbled Himself to share our humanity, Your Son Jesus Christ; who lives and reigns with You, in the unity of the Holy Spirit, one God, for ever and ever. *Amen.*

APPENDIX

THE APOSTLES' CREED

I believe in God the Father Almighty,
Maker of heaven and earth:

And in Jesus Christ His only Son, our Lord,
Who was conceived by the Holy Ghost,
Born of the Virgin Mary,
Suffered under Pontius Pilate,
Was crucified, dead, and buried:
He descended into hell;
The third day He rose again from the dead;
He ascended into heaven,
And sitteth at the right hand of God the Father Almighty;
From thence He shall come to judge the quick and the dead.

I believe in the Holy Ghost;
The holy catholic church;
The communion of saints;
The forgiveness of sins;
The resurrection of the body;
And the life everlasting.
Amen.

THE LORD'S PRAYER

Our Father, who art in heaven,

Hallowed be Thy name.

Thy Kingdom come,

Thy will be done on earth as it is in heaven.

Give us this day our daily bread

And forgive us our debts, as we forgive our debtors.

And lead us not into temptation,

But deliver us from evil,

For Thine is the Kingdom, and the power, and the glory, forever. *Amen.*

A WAY OF PERSONAL EXAMINATION

Consider God's holiness and grace, manifest in the life of the Son, Jesus Christ.

Pray for God's presence and illumination. Ask God's Spirit to be with you and for your eyes to be open as you consider your day.

> Examine yourself prayerfully:
>
> Search me, O God, and know my heart!
> Try me and know my thoughts!
> And see if there be any grievous way in me,
> and lead me in the way everlasting! (Psalm 139:23-24)
>
> Note the times throughout the day you have seen God at work in your circumstances and in your heart. Name those ways in which you have resisted God and His will.

Pray in deep gratitude for every sign of God's loving presence, and pray in sorrow, repenting of any place you have resisted His loving will.

Receive the Words of Assurance for the day, leaning on the promises and mercy of God.

Conclude in prayer, offering yourself body and soul, in your thoughts, words, and actions, as a living sacrifice to God, which is your spiritual worship.

NOTES

Made in the USA
Monee, IL
13 November 2020